Social Media Marketing Power Mindset

Learn The Online Digital Advertising Strategies That Can Help Grow Your Business, Network, And Influencer Brand on Facebook, Instagram, LinkedIn and Youtube.

Table of Contents

Disclaimer

<u>Legal Notice:</u>

This book is copyright protected. This book is only for personal use. You cannot amend, distribute, sell, use, quote or paraphrase any part, or the content within this book, without the consent of the author or publisher.

<u>Disclaimer Notice:</u>

Please note the information contained within this document is for educational and entertainment purposes only. All effort has been executed to present accurate, up to date, and reliable, complete information. No warranties of any kind are declared or implied. Readers acknowledge that the author is not engaging in the rendering of legal, financial, medical or professional advice. The content within this book has been derived from various sources. Please consult a licensed professional before attempting any techniques outlined in this book.

By reading this document, the reader agrees that under no circumstances is the author responsible for any losses, direct or indirect, which are incurred as a result of the use of information contained within this document, including, but not limited to, — errors, omissions, or inaccuracies.

Introduction

In our fast-paced world, it seems like we are more desperate for quality content and consumable media now more than ever. While some people are perfectly satisfied with taking in the same thing over and over again, many individuals in our society want new media that they can like and share with their friends. The key to this tidbit of information is that some of that content can be our own advertisements and marketing strategies for our personal brands.

If you've made your way to this book, you are likely a small business owner of some sort looking to grow your customer base via your social media following. This book will go over many different kinds of social media users, not just one specific type. So, whether you're someone with a plumbing company or the person that wants to be the next Kim Kardashian, the secrets you need to get through the complex world of social media will lie here in this book.

You might also be an individual that's a freelancer, looking to boost your client base. Through all the different things we have to grow our business as a freelancer, it seems as though our social media pages are going to be the best options. People like having a brand they can look to and trust to get quality products at prices that are reasonable. If you are willing to share your life on social media, then people will trust you and be more willing to buy into your products.

Also, some of your potential audience will be people looking to simply build their online profile and become social media influencer's. You could make hundreds of thousands of dollars simply by having a massive social media following. It's not easy to get there at first, as the world online is so massive you can easily get lost. But with the right mindset, and tools, anything is possible on the Internet.

This book offers an overview guide on how to gain more social media followers, but there will be more important information than just growing your following. Not only do you want to get more followers for your business, but you should strive to get to a place where that ends up equaling more website traffic. More people that start flooding your website, the more money you'll end up making later on.

You can shell out for paid online advertising on different websites, but organic marketing on social media is going to be very helpful in growing your business. We live in a world where advertisements are ubiquitous. On the one hand, it's good for marketers because there are so many opportunities for you to get your brand out there. On the other hand, people are slightly becoming used to advertisements, so it's more challenging to get them to buy into what you're trying to sell them than it used to be. Decades ago, you could pose your product, related to beauty or not, with an attractive woman in heels and red lipstick. That can still be done today, but you also have to go beyond just using this kind of imagery itself.

Once you've understood the way that you can use both paid and organic marketing to get more followers for your social media, you will start to realize that it can drive traffic to your website as well. We will discuss business leads and product sales in each section, so you understand the financial benefits of having a lot of social media followers.

This book is for business startups that are ready to hit the jackpot they've been waiting for. If you're someone that wants to grow a company that makes them passive income, this is where you start. Anyone that is launching an app, clothing store or anything else that will solely be operated through the Internet needs to know the importance of using paid and organic marketing to get your brand out there and have a positive impact on society.

More and more people are choosing to open their own business or start freelancing. In our demanding capitalist society, we have to do whatever it takes to ensure that we're going to be making money and setting ourselves apart from other people that wish to do the same. The idea of having your own company or brand and making money off of that is a dream for many that will never be followed through. Now is your time to take back your life and start your own company. The best way to make sure that it thrives is going to be through social media marketing.

Social media has allowed us also to market ourselves and a brand that we created around who we are. Never before have we been able to profit so much from our own personality. You can take pictures of yourself holding products, or appearing in different places, and that can be what ends up making you thousands. Many people are able to launch their own brands or collaborate with others once they've grown a large following on their own personal social media pages as well.

You might not want just to brand yourself but become a major influencer in your industry or niche. This could include something as broad as cooking, to something more specific like a nail artist. The beauty of social media is that we've been able to take our art forms or the things that separate us from the rest of society, and we can profit from that. To be a famous chef used to mean having to get on a Food Network show or competing against others. Now, you can grow your brand all with the power of your phone.

Throughout the book, we are going to be looking at the top four places that you should create a social media platform on and how they can benefit you. All social media, in general, is going to be beneficial for your business, but you might be skeptical of some versus others, and that's completely fine. You should know that there is some crossover with the types of people that use them, and all forms of social media offer you unique ways that you can grow your business and get more marketing.

If you get on Facebook, you are exposing yourself to the largest social media platform. Though Facebook isn't what it seemed to be a while ago, especially for organic marketing, you still will have the opportunity to connect yourself with other people that are most interested in your product or service. Remember that this is a global market as well. Facebook isn't limited just to your state or country. You can reach specific groups and target more niche groups of people than you would be able to without social media. Facebook is relatively cheap to market on if you're going to be doing paid posts as well. Any form of social media is going to be good at building a clientele and creating loyalty between you and your customers. They will like having the ability to interact with the people in charge of providing the things they love.

Instagram is a great tool for anyone to market themselves towards as well. It started as an app that you could use to take beautiful pictures, but now, it's a way that you can successfully market your company. Instagram is different than other social media sites because it allows things to be presented more creatively. You can post a video, photo set, or live stream of anything you want. You can interact with your followers by posting likes, and Instagram stories lets you run polls and quizzes. Being more interactive with followers means that you can create higher quality products and services. Not only will you get closer to your client base, but you will also be defining your brand and making more of an established image for yourself.

Youtube is becoming like the new TV. It's important that we take advantage of this free service. Youtube has almost five billion views a day. With Youtube ads, you get to target like you might on Facebook or Instagram. You can specifically hit certain demographics using keywords and categories based on certain Internet searches.

Chapter 1 – Why is Social Media Marketing Helpful for Businesses And Brands?

Many of us can remember a time when we first heard about a social media platform from a friend. To share your feelings used to mean that you would have to create some form of art, maybe a poem or a song. Now, with the use of social media, we've been given the ability to go online and write a simple post expressing the mood that we've been in that day. That's only social media on its simplest level, too. Imagine someone creating a post-it note of their thoughts, posting it on the wall at work for everyone to see. Then they expect those walking by to like what they've said, maybe leave a comment. Implementing social media into the real world has been an adjustment, but we didn't waste any time acclimating the world of advertising with the use of social media.

In today's world, social media is ubiquitous and certainly not going away anytime soon. Everywhere you go, there are signs in shop windows telling you to "like" something on social media, a newly branded hashtag on the bottom of our receipts, and even social media symbols popping up on the products that we choose to use. Those that still reject social media are quickly becoming outcasts, and very few people will remain free of having at least one personal social media platform. It's almost a survival tool now. Not everyone needs to have a social media account, but to break into a lucrative world for your brand and business, you're doing yourself a disservice not immersing yourself into at least one major social media network.

However, it can be tricky to balance out your social media presence, because those that openly use social media too much - or worse over-brand themselves - can become seemingly out of touch very quickly in the online world. What's most anxiety-inducing to remember is that a lot of what you decide to put online will stay there.

Now, Facebook, Instagram, Youtube, and LinkedIn all have different types of visitors that respond to certain marketing materials in a myriad of different ways. As we go through this book, however, you'll start to see that the best option doesn't lie within just one social platform, but within all of them. That's the beauty of social media. You don't have to stick with just one. They all exist, are free to sign up with, and some even work very well together.

Those who don't see the power they have with the opportunities social media has handed to them are missing out on a huge chance to expand the business and grow a large and loyal following.

To count every person in the world would be impossible. Some people you might have thought were dead; others were never listed as being born. As quick as you can take a record of someone's life, more people will have died, and even more, will have been born. We will only come in contact with a fraction of these people in our lives. If we're lucky enough to travel, we might see more people than those that don't leave their homes often.

But when you get on the Internet, you unlock the ability to connect with more people than you could ever hope to meet in your life. Just think of the influencer's who have over a million followers. They could never have the time to meet those people. And yet 1 million users still know all about - and follow - their lives, comment on their posts, and reach out to them like an old friend.

There are an estimated 7.7 billion people in the world. Out of those, there are about 5 billion that use cell phones, and 4/5 of those people use the Internet. It's safe to say that at least half the people alive are using the Internet on their cell phones, which means they likely do on computers as well. These people are most likely young adult users, and the people that don't use cell phones and the Internet are likely children and the elderly that don't have or need access to cell phones as often as others do.

Finally, around 3 billion of these individuals will have a social media account. Having a social media account doesn't mean all of your personal information is online. All of this is hard to process on an accessibility level, but the point is, that social media has made interacting with others easier than ever. You can do almost anything with the power of the Internet.

Theoretically speaking, then, this means that if you market via social media, 3 billion people will have access to your brand globally.

Quick side note; we will be using the term 'brand' as an all-encompassing, blanket term that will refer to whichever product, service, or idea you intend to market on social media.

Now, you might be reading this book as a business owner, or perhaps as an aspiring social influencer who wants to grow a significant following. Whatever it may be that you want to achieve, your goal will be to have a brand that matters, including a good product, a meaningful message, or positive lifestyle influence. These are what help give people a brand that they'll want to follow and buy into.

This means that even if .01 percent of the people online saw your product, that's still 100,000 people, roughly. Even if you have a social media presence, you might not be able to succeed without the right tactics.

But if you don't try at all, however, then you're not going to have any success. The only way to achieve what you want is to start on the right track with a successful social media strategy.

The Growth of The Internet And Social Media

It's estimated that the number of Internet users grows by around 7 percent each year. And in less than two decades, the number of cell phone users will be double what it is now, which is an astonishing number.

Cell phones are becoming more accessible and creating social media accounts is more desirable. They seemed to just be a life enhancement at one point, but now, they're the life source for many individuals. We all know that one person that would seemingly die if they didn't have their phone glued to their pocket. There's always a person we follow online that seems like they over-share, making us question if they are struggling in their real life as much as they seem to be, or if it's just a result of too much social media use.

Our world demands that we stay in touch. Innovations emerge overnight, and everyone is more desperate now than ever for advancement. It seems strange to think that we used to have women dying regularly from childbirth when we're at such an advanced medical level in the western world. At the same time, it also seems confusing that we have yet to discover a clearer, less static-filled way of communicating on the phone. The release of a new iPhone means that we'll toss our old ones in the trash in a heartbeat. We admire cars from decades ago, but a phone that is more than five years old seems like an offense to our technological sensibilities.

All of this growth causes us to look at marketing on a global platform in a way that is much more accessible than it used to be. To start to grow your brand a few decades ago, you might have had to buy an ad in the newspaper or hope that you could save money to get a spot on the local

TV or radio station. You'd reach out to only those that were around you.

And rather than tap into a wide community interested in your brand, your ad might have only extended as far as a fifty-mile radius. Yet in just a few short decades, we've advanced to a point where you have the ability to easily find customers online and interact with them, whether it's through a Facebook group or a niche Instagram page.

Connecting with people globally has never been easier, and from now on, we can guarantee that as long as our society continues to grow and put an emphasis on innovation, it will only get easier. Now, you can create an Instagram account and get followers overnight. The level of success you will find within your strategies will certainly differ, but at the end of the day, it's much easier to market your brand now than it used to be.

Using different types of social media should be your goal, but for now, we're going to get into specifics about the different kinds of social media and who uses what the most.

For example, you might find that your brand does better on Facebook than it does on Instagram right now, so you should look for ways to improve on that. Rather than placing an emphasis solely on Facebook, we'll give you ways that you can improve your Instagram even if you have less than ten followers right now.

You'll soon see, by the end of this book, that putting yourself on multiple platforms is going to be your best option. We'll discuss that throughout this book.

Now, the chapter on Facebook will be the longest because we'll give you some basic marketing tips, like the types of ads you should be using and what pictures do the best for different kinds of companies. There's a lot of psychology that goes into studying how people react to different marketing strategies, so it's important to know that there's more than just luck and exposure when putting ads out there.

The growth of social media allows anything to be possible. It sometimes can feel like trying to win the lottery when navigating social media. You're just hoping for that one post to go viral or get the picture with the most likes on your feed. Many hope to get the attention of someone notable or to be featured on a celeb's sponsored Instagram post. Whatever you desire with your social media marketing, you understand the struggle of nothing working online. That's why you made it here. Only, your online profile isn't going to be dependent on chance alone. That's how it's completely different from the lottery. You can make it happen. With the right knowledge, dedication, and understanding of how social media and the marketing process works, you can navigate the vastly growing online world.

Social media isn't going away, and that's seen in the numbers. It makes some people wonder what the rush is then? If Facebook is still around for another decade, then why is there this urgency to get on now? Wouldn't it be easier to start out later, when there are 10 billion users? The answer might seem like yes, but actually, it's much more important to make sure you're getting on now. It can take some brands a few years to get settled on social media after trial and error periods of what their followers like. As more people are getting on board, you don't want to be the last one to join. It becomes harder to find originality as more and more copies are made.

Think about the greatest song you've ever heard, and how many thereafter came out that sounded similar to that one great hit. We can estimate that around 100 million songs have been "officially" released, though who knows how many might be floating around on mix-tapes and burned CDs. But that's not the point. The reason for this comparison is that many songs seem to sound the same. It's more common now to hear a reproduced tune than it is to listen to that one great hit. At any given time, it seems like there are at least a few songs on the radio that don't sound much different from each other. While there are an endless amount of note arrangements and melodies that can be created, other musicians get too influenced by what they already know, and originality can be forgotten. The same seems to be happening with social media brands. You can easily find five different beauty pages that sell various products, all resembling the same sort of minimalist, soft pink and white aesthetic that "natural" brands like Glossier have. Many fitness pages will have the same sort of black background with a shiny athlete working hard with some sort of variation on a motivational quote underneath. The longer you wait, the harder it will be to establish your own unique voice rather than falling into one of many similar categories.

Now, think of how there are billions of people on the Internet, and only more expected to pop up in the coming years. If you don't establish your brand, product, service, or whichever it is that you're marketing, you might get lost among billions of others in the future. Now is the time to get online and brand yourself in order to start establishing yourself right now before it's too late.

The Purpose Behind Social Media

The original intention of social media was for connections. It was a new form of communication. We've been searching for innovative ways to communicate since we started developing languages in the first place.

Now, the Internet has become a way of life. Not only can you talk to someone else whenever you want, but you can also order food, clothing, furniture, schedule doctors' appointments, flirt with singles, binge-watch entire series, and so much more. Part of our communicable world involves talking to the person next to you, but now, there's more of a focus on talking to people all across the world.

National communication first started with messengers that would carry important information physically or verbally, on foot or horseback. Eventually, a mail system started forming, and radio and telegraph systems led the way into phones. Now, we can open a small box we grabbed from our pockets and send crucial messages within seconds. And you can go online and chat with someone from a different part of the country.

Most of the time, we still use our personal social media for reaching out to just our family and close friends. But knowing we have an option to reach out further can be very powerful.

The communication barrier even seems lessened by the Internet as well. Memes are a common way that people can interact and relate to each other without having to know each other's native languages. Those that do speak different languages that want to talk can use online translators with ease as well. The purpose of social media, in the beginning, was communication. The purpose of it now is still communication. News channels communicate the breaking stories. Celebrities communicate their actions and feelings. Most importantly, brands can communicate their messages and reach the clients, customers, and users that they have been wanting.

People still use these phones for important purposes such as communication. But now, the whole time they're on their phone, they're also bombarded with advertisements and messages from companies that want them to buy into their products. Marketing is more accessible than ever before, but it's also a bit challenging to go about it in a successful way. Because we can't look anywhere without being sold something, our brains are getting better at shutting certain things out. When the commercials start playing on Hulu, you can mute and pull your phone out. If an ad is playing on Snapchat or Instagram stories, you're trained to swipe right away. As marketers, we have to look at how we ignore ads ourselves and put an emphasis on the ones that grab our attention. What is it about them that's able to make us want to buy something without even prompting the ad to sell us that thing in the first place? This is going to be the most important thing to remember throughout this book. As you create your ads, ask yourself, *how do I make this ad stand out from the rest?*

Still, the best kind of advertisement and marketing has always been word of mouth and now were able to do that online, sometimes even for free. Simply "liking" a movie on Facebook lets your friends know that you give that movie a positive recommendation. Rather than having to invite a friend to your favorite brunch spot, you can simply follow their page on Instagram and let all your followers see that it's a place you like and that they should go there. "Word of mouth" has transformed in a way that social media marketers can take more active control. Not only will word of mouth be dependent on having a good product in the first place, but you'll also need to make sure that your content is something shareable that people enjoy following as well.

Chapter 2 – Why Is Social Media So Effective At Capturing (And Keeping) Our Attention?

When social media first started dominating culture over a decade ago, it seemed like some sites were passing fads just used by teenagers. Many saw these kids as desiring to fill their time and connect with others, with some social media sites having a high turnover.

Facebook seemed to replace Myspace and AOL messenger, and soon we expected something like Twitter and Instagram to replace Facebook. Instead, they all just started to work together, and eventually, bought into each other giving us features that work across multiple platforms. Many people will log into one or more social media platforms a day. This means that if you are on multiple platforms, you have a higher chance of influencing more than just one person.

Now, well over a decade since its launch back in 2004, it seems as though Facebook is just as popular as ever before. Rather than turning to new social media platforms, we just add them to the others that already exist. What is it that helps keep audiences glued to their phone screens? In order to figure out why people enjoy using social media so much, we have to look at why we do ourselves.

Make a list of every reason that you get on social media. Maybe it's to look at the news or keep in touch with siblings from across the country. Perhaps you enjoy seeing what your college classmates are up to now, or maybe you like looking at the plates at the restaurants in your local area. Whatever it may be, figure out why you enjoy logging on yourself, and you'll start to realize that many of your followers likely have these same reasons as well.

It seems in our world that people like consistency. Many people work 9-5 jobs, every weekend and holiday spent with family, grilling or eating some other sort of tradition-based food. Every year, the leaves fall, and the winter holidays come back around.

Yet as the snow melts away, so do our layers of on-brand fashion styles all of which change year to year. Though conformity and regulation are seen all around us, humans are still desperate for change. The key to having the right social media account is giving people the consistency they want while also ensuring that you're providing the innovation needed for their interest to keep up.

If you stay the same forever, then people will start to seek out change elsewhere. While many people are still fine with doing the same thing over and over again, they will be more adaptable to change than they would be comfortable with things never becoming different. For example, every time an app seems to update, people get upset, saying how they don't like the new feature. Eventually, everyone gets over it and repeats the same thing when there's a new update.

If Facebook hadn't updated since it first emerged, there would likely be very few people still using the platform. We all have those friends that complain when a site changes too much, but normally, very few users actually drop off the social media app.

Thats because people not only crave change, but they become more accepting of it as well, ready and waiting for new updates that fix the old things they don't like. Remember this when creating your brand and logo. You have to come up with something that alters through time and evolves for the better in order to keep up with trends and your client's needs and wants. With so much competition out there, you have to stay just as relevant as ever, ensuring the thrill of a new brand doesn't take over your follower's desires to move onto the next.

These apps are so powerful and ubiquitous because they are psychologically defined to be. There are teams of marketers and people that work with users and focus groups to determine what's working and what's not. A lot of money is invested in study and research of people and how they operate on social media in order for the various platform users to get a better grasp on how they can improve the lives of their clients. On some level, that can seem kind of scary. A lot of power can come for those that are able to manipulate their followers and find ways to control their spending decisions.

But remember, your intention shouldn't be to try to take advantage of others. Rather, you should focus on finding ways to make your brand stand out from everyone else. People have a lot of options as to how to spend their time and money, especially once they get online. Make your brand the top choice for your potential customers by becoming a brand they can depend on.

Some things aren't around because they're good, but simply because we've come to accept them as a society. It's time for brands to find new ways of innovation, and it seems like social media is helping them to do so. In order to get in on this fast-paced marketing innovation, we have to understand the psychology of social media use.

The Psychology Behind Social Media Usage

At any given time, you might check social media and see a bright red mark, circle, +1, or other symbol notifying that you have something to check up on. Whether it's a message, friend request, update, or other notification, we constantly check our social media because of that tiny little alert. That's called a 'call to action'.

That little plus symbol or the number one is letting you know that your attention is needed. What might be waiting on the other side of that notification might be something exciting, that could change your day. Perhaps a new love interest just messaged you, or maybe you won a contest that you entered a while ago. Either way, that little red alert is taking your attention and putting an emphasis on something that you need to do.

When you are creating a brand and a social media platform, remember to incorporate notifications in the process. Giving someone a reason to take time out of their day and put it towards you is enough to make them think about your brand. You don't want to be annoying about it, spamming their in-boxes with general messages. Still, a comment on their photograph or a unique and specific message reaching out to them can be what they need to feel as though you were going out of your way to make them feel important.

Another level of the psychology behind why we use social media is general conformity. The idea that everyone else is doing something so we should to, still applies to social media. If every one of your friends is on Instagram and you aren't, there will be times where you feel left out in conversations. They might reference a picture or social media influencer unknown to those that aren't online, and there's a general feeling of being left out that can be hard to handle. This is why a lot of people might even get on social media in the first place, only to let it become a part of their life once they've become used to the functions.

This is an important bit of psychological information to remember when you're creating your social media pages. You want to ensure that you are giving your followers a reason to feel like they need to join in the trend.

The bandwagon is one of the most classic marketing techniques, and we need to remember it when creating our social media marketing strategy.

Perhaps you could share news updates that give your followers shareable content. Whatever it may be, finding something that will give followers a reason to go to your page is crucial in creating noteworthy content.

Some scientists use the idea of social media to explain "social capital" among teens and other young adults. Social capital is like the money that keeps the "bank" open, known as society.

What's popular and what's dated is identified and labeled within a society to let others know what should be bought into and what should be ignored. Those that are at the top of the ladder in terms of social capital are also the ones that set the trends.

For example, Kim Kardashian is one of the most followed people on Instagram, and whenever she posts a picture in a new dress, there are companies that will rip that design off and market it to their customers.

Many individuals will try to copy some of Kim's looks as a form of adding to their own social capital. We use social media as a means of determining where we fit in this society and what we give out in a certain social setting as well.

Social capital used to present itself through clothes, cars, and houses. What you wore, where you lived, the kind of car you drove, and who you hung out and dated were all important in order to place you on a certain level in society.

Of course, not everyone plays into these ideas and will very much try to separate themselves from the institutions that bind us. Still, we have to remember the things that keep us operating in a society and what forms of social capital we use.

While those things like cars and clothes are still very much a part of our society, social networking is a new kind of exchange. How many followers you have can be more important than what your job level might be. The number of likes and comments you get on a picture might be indicative of your social state in a certain setting as well. Whether this kind of stuff is important to you or not doesn't really matter. As a marketer, it's important to know that it's still a way many people base their perspectives on social status.

This means creating standards for your brand beyond just what is expected. While you might find that you get more followers by following thousands of people, constantly liking and commenting on others posts, you'll soon discover that it doesn't give you as much social capital as limiting your use might.

Brands that let the followers come to them and don't reach out as much don't look as desperate, meaning that they have other desirable qualities that put them higher on the social ladder.

In order for us to be psychologically satisfied, we need to have a level of identity. Your identity is who you are and how you fit into the world. The things you like and what you choose to do is all very important in defining your identity. This is created by us, usually encompassing the ideas of others on a certain level.

Your identity is based on the things that you were taught as you grew up. What was "cool" and what was not was defined throughout your teen years. And going through college as a young adult helped give you new perspectives and defined your beliefs.

Not everyone will have a solid identity or idea of who they are deep down, but we are all still consistently trying to discover what that identity is. Humans love labeling things because it makes it easier to process. We do this to ourselves as well. Social media now plays a crucial part in helping us identify who we are.

As a marketer, it's going to be important to remember this psychological tidbit. People are going to want to identify themselves, and sometimes, that will mean using your brand. Give them something that they can use as a tool to home in on who they are and that helps them become the person that they want to be.

We have a desire to seek validation in order to ensure our emotions are important. When you're feeling upset, it feels a lot better when the people around you validate you and remind you that you aren't wrong for being upset. We have to ensure that what we feel makes sense so that we have healthy responses and emotional reactions to different situations.

Social media can provide us with that validation as well. When you're feeling lonely or bored, you can get online and see that others are feeling the same way. Memes are funny ways that remind us that other people have similar feelings to ours. When you're creating a brand that people will implement into their lives, give them validation. Create content that is honest and relatable. Don't be a robot and show that your company has emotions just like everyone else, and that you're there to make connections and offer solutions.

Social media gives people a sense of control in an otherwise chaotic world. Now, while not every person in the world wants to be in charge, we all wish to have a certain level of power. We look for this power in our jobs, and home lives, the way we act and the way that we dress. Some people are more power hungry than others, and plenty of individuals are satisfied with letting others take the wheel.

When we get online and start creating social media platforms, you can find that you now have the ability to manipulate emotions and garner responses in a quantitative way. The world at large looks to social media for answers for the thoughts that seem to be out of our control.

So when creating a marketable brand and successful company, remember this desire for control in your audience. Give your followers the opportunity to have a sense of power in relation to your brand. You can do this by posting polls, asking questions, and even by responding to some criticism as well.

Chapter 3 – The Power of Facebook (And How To Use It To Grow Your Business or Brand)

Facebook has a little less than 1.5 billion users. When looking at a number like that, you might get a little overwhelmed. Not 1 million, but 1 billion! That's hundreds and hundreds of millions of users.

Each day, a portion of these people log on and see advertisements that they click on. A portion of those people can be individuals that see your ad as well. You might not have even close to a million followers at the moment, but that doesn't mean you can't eventually get there with the right effort.

We have to also take note of the power each individual Facebook user has as well. While one person might scroll past your page, another could end up spending $1,000 in one purchase. Luckily, Facebook gives us important analytics to look at these kinds of statistics as well so we can determine if what we're doing is successful or not.

Every year, Facebook contributes to over 20 billion ad clicks. Not only are these ads seen that many times and more, but these are direct clicks to websites, products, and whatever else that's being advertised.

Someone might see your ad, and later in the day go on your website directly themselves. Just because you're not getting direct ad clicks doesn't mean that people won't be still using your product or service or that you won't be benefiting from their sales.

For example, picture 10 people logging onto Facebook, all of them seeing your ad. One person might click right away. Another scrolls past and ends up seeing your ad again, only to click on it then. Four people scroll past and ignore it, and four people remember your brand name, two of them heading independently to your site at later times in the week. Just because you only got one click right away, that doesn't mean your ad post still didn't reach other people.

Still, Facebook fan pages aren't reaching customers as much as they used to. There was a crackdown on what content could be posted on Facebook, and a lot of companies found that their content was filtered out of the Facebook feed, which meant that their Facebook posts didn't reach very many people.

However, with billions of active users, it's easy to see that Facebook is still very relevant in the social media world. It's not about giving up on Facebook because new results are different. Instead, we just have to find ways to navigate around it.

Fortunately, we have analytics and statistics that can help us determine when the best time to post is, and who is most often viewing your advertisements.

People don't use Facebook as often as they used to, but that doesn't mean there are necessarily fewer accounts. It is up to the users to keep it active and relevant, and using more niche, and specific Facebook groups and pages will be helpful in making sure that we still connect to the right audience.

Groups are important not just for Facebook, but for Youtube and LinkedIn as well. You want your company to be open and accessible, but there also has to be a level of exclusion that you use with certain clients because they seek out that type of treatment.

Facebook groups are a great way to get your brand a direct audience that's more likely to respond when you post new content. Your Facebook group can also be closed to new members, making it feel all the more exclusive.

Most importantly, we have to remember that Facebook is still free to use. That's all there is to it. When we have some form of marketing available to us, we have to use it. There are audiences on Facebook that you might not connect to elsewhere.

Using free social media is like stapling your "Garage Sale" sign on a street post. It's something that people are used to seeing, and when it's relevant to them, they will notice. All the while, you are paying almost nothing for marketing.

What Is Facebook?

When Facebook was first created, it was actually known as FaceMash. It was created by Mark Zuckerberg in 2003 with the help of his roommate Eduardo Saverin. Mark Zuckerberg is now worth over 60 billion dollars.

For the full story on how this started, you can watch the movie about it called *The Social Network*. A lot has still changed since that time, so it will be interesting to see if there will be another installment to this riveting story. That kind of money is the level where you can do whatever you want because you simply have enough money to do so. None of that means Mark Zuckerberg will be stopping any time soon, either. Instead, he hopes to bring more to the customers and users of Facebook so that people continue to use it and more individuals will choose to sign up.

It all started as a platform for university students, specifically Harvard and other prestigious school attendees. Then, more and more users got on, and now Facebook is a global network in which people share everything from what they had for lunch, to the news of a family member's death. Though you might have college friends on Facebook, that usually isn't the only purpose it exists anymore. It helps us be reminded of individuals' birthdays, and there's a feature that shows you the pictures and activities you did on a certain day so many years ago.

There have been marriage announcements, fights between ex-lovers, and even live-streamed weddings on Facebook. It can be anything, and it's all up to the user that has the account. With so much power comes a lot of use and desire to stay relevant and updated on the app. There are many changes coming in the months and years ahead, and Facebook's head-honchos know what they need to do to remain relevant.

Much of the innovation is going to be seen through the ads that become available on Facebook. One of these great features will be the ability to add stickers to story modes of Facebook.

Another feature developing will be the ability to "try on" products and give the users a chance to see for themselves what a certain makeup or clothing item will look like on before they decide to make the purchase. Facebook is a great place for companies to have a page that shares updates and news about their products. In 2019, recommendations were added to allow businesses the opportunity to let their customers share positive reviews with their friends.

Chapter 4 – How to Use Facebook Organic Marketing to Grow Your Business or Brand

Organic marketing is a reference to the natural reach of a social media post without requiring paid advertising.

This could include having a business or professional profile page and posting regular pictures, videos, and status updates. These types of organic marketing materials will only be seen by those that already follow you, and the people that they might choose to share your information with. It won't pop up randomly on other people's pages and doesn't have to include a sponsored notification anywhere because it is a regular post like any other account. It is encompassing of the chances or likelihood that someone is going to see your post as it naturally appears on their feed.

At any given time, you can get on Facebook and see a different arrangement of posts based on an algorithm Facebook uses to show you what you want. Your goal with organic marketing will be to provide people with the content that will be frequently included in their algorithm.

This organic reach includes factors such as how often you post, the time that you post, how popular your posts are, and how many posts you have versus how many others have on a particular user's page.

A person that has 1,000 friends and likes 500 pages has a lot less of a chance of seeing your post than a person with 100 friends that doesn't like anything. While you can't control what others have in their feeds, you can control whether or not your content is something that *they want* in their feed.

In Mark Zuckerberg's attempt to help users only see ads that have more meaningful purposes and help elicit connections, this organic reach was limited and caused it to drop to as low as 2%.

Changes like these can be scary because it could mean money lost for certain businesses. The thing to remember, however, is that organic reach will never fully be gone.

The main thing to remember about organic reach is the need for <u>quality</u> content over <u>quantity</u>. So before you start to think that you should frequently post throughout the day, remember that the more you post, the more of a chance there is for a certain ad to get lost in the Facebook feeds of your audience.

Having a few good quality posts is going to be a lot more helpful to your content getting noticed than if you post 100 times a day every 5 minutes.

In order to get business leads that eventually lead to website traffic and product sales, you have to ensure that you're posting quality that is worthy of being shared. On top of that, it should engage with the audience.

Something that encourages conversation will be the most successful. You might have seen articles in your feed that are very controversial, or even easily proved wrong and make you question, "why would someone post that?" Well, for a while, controversial posts like biased articles or sexist pieces were getting the most traffic because everyone would comment angry things and get into fights with strangers on the Internet.

The people that commented on the article shared that post to all of their friends, helping it to go viral. Soon, however, Facebook noticed this type of 'click-bait' content, and cut back on the types of posts they would allow on their platform. So making sure your content is engaging is still important, only as long as it falls within Facebook's guidelines.

Note, it's not the process of getting business leads on Facebook that's challenging. The hard part will be putting an interesting ad out there, one that makes people want to interact with your content.

Posting about one a day is a good daily target. And if not once a day, at least 4 to 5 times a week. Anything less won't be enough to keep users engaged, and more than that will start to feel like spam. A person might have access to every single one of your ads, always seeing your new content in their feed.

While that's good for you, it could be annoying for them to see similar ads five times in a row when they just logged onto Facebook just to see pictures of their baby niece.

It's All About Edutainment (Educational Entertainment)

Creating high-quality Facebook posts is central to Facebook marketing success, so it's important to understand what that means for your Facebook content. First and foremost, this means high-quality with aesthetics.

People will judge your post immediately based on the image that is shared. So you should feature clear images, not things that are blurry or cut off.

Your grammar needs to be correct, and it should not be confusing or misleading. Anything that looks sloppy will seem unprofessional, and with so many scammers out there, no one is going to feel safe spending their money on a site that seems less than top-notch.

You will also need to give your user's a sense of meaning about your business or brand. This might include fulfilling a need, establishing identity, or simply being entertaining. Perhaps you're a plumbing company, giving people useful information about how to properly care for their pipes during the freezing season. Though you're not directly selling your services, you're giving the users meaning.

You're identifying a problem and giving them a solution, providing them with interesting information that they will remember along with your brand. Establishing an identity might be done with a clothing or music brand. You might post images of your models wearing clothes with a simple caption, "who's ready for the weekend?" People see these models and envision the weekend, feeling good and commenting, liking, or sharing the post.

Entertainment is also going to be a great way to market yourself organically on Facebook. Sharing a funny picture or meme can have others sharing your post with their friends. For example, if you own a bakery, you might share a picture of your freshly frosted cupcakes along with a popular meme that says something like, "my face when I see these cupcakes." Don't use that exactly, but you get the point. Giving users content that they would see from their friends is the high-quality stuff that they'll want.

To get the best website traffic on a consistent level, there will be some testing involved on your part. Start by posting every day for a week and see which days get the most traffic to your website. Once you've determined this, you should start to see patterns among different days of the week, so you can keep that in mind for the next step. Now, it's time for you to try a few different marketing strategies with your posts each day this week.

Videos are going to be the best way for you to reach out to your audience. Videos are eye-catching and engaging. The best kind of consumable ad for users, video or not, is one that both entertains them and one that is educational. Reading is important and will always be relevant, but when people are on their work breaks or scrolling their phone at school, they don't want to read a long post. Instead, they're more likely to stop for a video. A video with interesting sound is important, but if you can convey your message without audio, that's when you'll really start to get people watching. Think of Buzzfeed Tasty videos. Rather than listing a recipe or having someone explain how to do it, they have quick videos that show directly how to create something, and their followers love this formula.

Quick side note, be careful (when posting on Facebook) that you don't directly encourage your users to "like," "share," and "comment", as this goes against Facebook's rules.

This rule is one that is specifically for Facebook, because they are careful about what ads might be shared with their users. Still, it's important to remind your users that they should "subscribe" to you, whether that's through liking your page or following you.

However, if you do it too much, Facebook has an algorithm that will automatically filter this content out of your follower's feeds as an attempt to clean up too many ads from one person's page.

When it comes to getting more people to see your ads and click on them, it's all about timing. Some marketers will try to get tricky, thinking that posting at night means it's the first thing users see in the morning. While there are some tricks you might find as you post more for your own page, remember to start simple.

Posts are most shared on Saturdays first, and Sundays after that. During the week, Wednesdays are popular days as well. Try posting between 7pm and 10pm, depending on where you are in a certain time zone.

This is when people are going to be winding down and scrolling their phones after work or while watching TV.

Once you hit these major times, you can start to find that there are different periods that are good for you to post. For example, if you're an alcohol brand and most of your followers are people that party, then posting on Monday at 8 am won't be the best time. Perhaps you're a natural baby product company, and many stay-at-home moms follow you, so the time you would decide to post would have to be different.

If You Reach Them, They Will Buy

Product sales will start once a consistent level of website traffic has been reached. This is what it's all about in the end for many different users. Even though some of you reading this might be influencer's looking to grow their brand rather than people that are specifically selling a product, like a clothing item or a meal at a restaurant.

The first step in successful marketing and good product sales is to actually have a quality product that people want to buy. You might be able to use smoke and mirrors at first to make money from a product quickly, but if it's not good, eventually, the sales will stop. Social media gives users a voice, and your product could get destroyed by a certain number of unhappy users.

Once you have established a quality product and the website traffic starts coming in, that's when you'll see product sales. At first, more people might be willing to try something out. Eventually, you might start to see sales drop. That is why it's important for you to have a long-term strategy to ensure that the customers you already have will keep coming back.

The beauty of social media, however, is that you are going to be able to interact with users, consumers, and customers to determine how to make your product better. You can take advice from your customers, run polls, and interact with the audience via your social media platform - all of which can help you create a specific product that people love. So when a customer is unhappy, listen to their complaints and help them find a happy solution rather than lose an angry customer.

Consider curating other peoples content as a way of organic marketing. Sharing the posts of another business or brand could help both of you reach out to new audiences that you wouldn't have sold to in the first place!

The best kind of marketing on social media is the kind of marketing that isn't blatantly selling you something. So be careful about posting content that intentionally states you're trying to get people to click on your link, go to your website, or buy your products.

Customers like to think that it was their idea to buy a product, so they might look at someone's dress and ask where it was purchased, making them more likely to buy this item of clothing than if they were originally told, "buy this dress here."

Give people a reason to like your page in the first place. Fulfill their need of some sort. Give them the content that they're used to, what they know and love, while still providing something new and interesting that they can't find elsewhere. People need a payoff for a lot of the things they do.

Share your other social media pages. We won't include this in the other sections, but it goes for all forms of social media. You should have your Facebook link in your Twitter bio and share your screen-shots of tweets on your Facebook page. Give your users accessible links so that they know how to best reach you in multiple different ways.

Chapter 5 – How to Use Facebook Paid Marketing to Grow Your Business or Brand

As a social media user yourself, you might think that there's no way people get that much sales revenue by running Facebook ads.

You yourself probably see 2o+ ads a day in your own personal Facebook feed. And maybe, at most, you'll click on just 1 or 2 of those ads.

But remember, you're just one of the thousands of people that see that ad. So, while there's a five percent chance that you might click on an ad, there's a five percent chance users will click on an ad, meaning potentially 50 out of 1000 people.

Actually, Facebook is going to make close to 4 billion dollars this year from Facebook ads alone. This is money that they make from people that pay to have their content posted, so whether you make more or less from what you post is going to be directly related to your brand and your sales.

Still, Facebook does what they have to in order to ensure that users don't leave their site right away when clicking on an ad. If someone clicks on your ad, they might get a pop up that says something like, "you're about to leave Facebook, are you sure you want to do this?" It is your mission, then, to make sure that you are giving your followers a reason to actually click out of Facebook and head to your site. This can't be done simply with an easy ad. Most people won't admit that they get on Facebook to shop. It is your job as an advertiser to get them to change their intentions once they see your post, especially when it is one that you are paying for.

Decide what the intention of your ad post is going to be. Is it to drive traffic to your website, or simply create brand awareness? Different types of ads will have different intentions behind them, and you should be aware of exactly what you want your ad to do for your business or brand.

Stand Out From The Competition By Using Facebook Ads

The most important thing you are going to get from your Facebook ads includes business leads, website traffic, and product sales. People will have to be interested in your post so that they actually click on it and learn more about your company. Then, when they are an active follower, they're likely going to head back to your website more often, leading to more product sales. The more you can encourage this, the easier it will be to get traffic to your site.

There are many different types of Facebook ads you can choose to use when starting your Facebook posts. These might include video, pictures, status updates, your website, lead generating ads, or simply your Facebook page as a whole.

Choose what is best for your company, not necessarily what's the most popular. A celebrity, an influencer, an icon, or a person branding themselves would want to promote their posts and their page in general. This is because you want people to relate to you so that they can later buy into the things you might be selling. People aren't going to be as likely to click a link to your website if they don't know who you are.

If you're a business, like a restaurant or a store, you would want to promote your pictures and your page. This way, you can get people to stay updated and follow what news your company might have. Links to your pages are important, but it's good that you are getting people interested in the brand at first, so they recognize it more as something they trust later on.

If your company is a service, getting them to your website is important. For example, a painting service isn't something people will need on a regular basis. It's more of a one and done kind of thing, and maybe in five or ten years when they need a new paint job, they'll come to you. Instead of getting people to like your page, a service company would probably do better with people going straight to their website.

Once you've determined the type of ad you want to run, it's time to figure out how best to put your ideas into a branded message.

Videos that engage your audience always do the best, as we discussed in the last section. All the rules we went over for organic marketing are going to be applicable to this kind of marketing as well. Just remember when you're paying for something, you want to get the message across quickly. Sell yourself within the first 3 seconds of a video, and make sure your article titles are on point (and, ideally, under 50 characters long).

Use catchy phrases in your headings and comments as well. Things like "did you know," or other forms of presenting information are important in getting readers interested. Stating facts and saying bold statements is also very helpful in keeping the attention of your audience.

When you've come up with the perfect ad, whether it's a video, picture, or post, it's time for you to determine who you're going to be marketing towards. At first, you may choose to advertise to the people in your local area, especially if you're a service-based company.

A store in California isn't going to do the best marketing towards New York individuals at first. Down the line, website sales might be a part of your business model, but that's going to be up to you to determine depending on your strategy.

Facebook ads gives you the option to choose whether or not you will reach out to the local community around you or focus on promoting yourself to people with specific targeted interests.

Using Facebook Ads Manager, you can choose to market towards people based on their location, age, gender, interest, and category. Age is important because offering baby items isn't going to be as successful towards elderly people and teenagers as it would be with young adults.

Gender is important too, because not only will marketing towards the right people be important, but you have to think of their friends as well and the likelihood that they might share your content with their friends.

When it comes to interest-based targeting - and using categories for your ads - there are a few things you should know before making a decision. Broad categories will include things like electronics, movie genres, and other hobbies. For example, if you run a Youtube channel posting video game tutorials and reviews, then you're probably going to have a better chance marketing to individuals in a gaming category focused interest, rather than targeting people that are closest to you geographically.

So start by determining what it is that you are selling, and who is going to do most of the buying. Then you can determine if there's a good category or interest that you can use.

There are other more specific targets as well, such as relationship status, if someone might be pregnant and expecting, if someone likes to travel a lot, or a person has an upcoming birthday. This type of hyper-personalization makes its easy to target your ad to your specific ideal audience.

Interest-targeting is based on the things that a Facebook user "likes" on their Facebook feed. Facebook ads then use that information to target ads towards their users.

This is much more specific in terms of how audiences might be targeted, but it will also provide the most returns in sales per ad click.

When you're first starting to create your brand and establish relationships with clients and customers, make sure you are using low-friction conversions. This would include asking them to sign up for a newsletter or "like" your page before trying to get them to buy something.

Avoid These Advertising Mistakes!

One of the biggest mistakes advertisers make on Facebook is choosing the wrong groups of people to target their ads towards. Many companies first start by finding the largest group of people possible and then placing their ads in front of them.

They think that the more people they reach, the more people will respond. However, this simply isn't the case. Many advertisers may think that this is the best approach, but they end up completely missing their target audience.

Specific interest-targeted ads may reach fewer people, but you will have a higher rate of return of clicks on your ads. That is what's most important, especially when you're shelling out money for the ad time on Facebook.

The next big mistake is when advertisers use the wrong images for their posts. The more unique you can get with your post, or more organic, rather, the better it will be.

Don't use recycled stock pictures that you've seen before. Avoid using your branded logo as well, unless people already know your image. It's usually best to try and create something personal that relates to people as much as their friend and families' pictures would.

The images that do the best for, when it comes to Facebook ads, are those that include people's faces in the frame. But try not to fall-back on the tired cliche of using images of sexy young women to capture your audiences attention.

Although this tacky tactic may have worked a decade ago, people are smarter than now and want something more authentic when it comes to ads on their social media feeds.

Be clear with what you're posting. If you have words in your pictures, don't use ten different fonts, or try to trick people into clicking on your image. Be upfront and honest and you'll find that this user-friendly method will have more people headed to your page.

Remember to keep a nice variety with your ads as well. You want more than one ad rotating at any given time, and it's important for you to make sure that the images you use are different enough to be attention-grabbing, yet familiar enough to chime with your overall brand.

Chapter 6 – The Power of Instagram (And How To Use It To Grow Your Business or Brand)

At first, it seemed as though Instagram was just a new way to share pictures, but in a more artistic way. Rather than uploading an album of ten or so different pictures from say your birthday party, on Instagram instead, you can simply choose one shot, the best shot.

At first, you could only post one picture, and it had to be a perfect square. This kind of image style helped Instagram develop its early signature brand.

Eventually, Instagram began allowing videos and pictures that could be longer and/or taller. And over time you could follow anyone who had a public profile, exchanging likes with them, and leaving comments on their posts.

Since its launch Instagram has transformed immensely, but high quality image content is still a key part of Instagram's content.

At first, Instagram was all about just taking selfies. Now, if you take a selfie while holding a bag of tea, and have a few thousand followers or more, you could actually make that your career, with some Instagram influencer's making thousands of dollars per post.

The different kinds of Instagram and the methods that people use to post on Instagram are varied, giving brands and people plenty of opportunities to sell themselves to their Instagram followers.

The most expensive Instagram post is estimated to be from Kylie Jenner, who does posts for close to a million dollars per sponsor. She's worked with companies like Fashion Nova and Sugar Bear Hair vitamins, who are two brands who do Instagram modeling with various celebrities and personalities.

It's clear to see that being a social media influencer can be very profitable, with the worldwide market for paid influencer sponsorships reaching close to a billion dollars, (and it is expected to double within just a couple of years!).

What started as a way to make extra money for some has become a desired dream for others. You don't have to become famous by singing, acting, or modeling anymore. Instead, you can simply snap a picture and gain a massive following, and then you can earn money per post on your profile.

While it's a tough market out there for those social media influencer's in the making, it's great for marketers because the options you have are almost endless.

Though people are more aware of paid sponsorships now, especially when companies are tagged and the hashtag #ad is being used, it is still a relevant market that can help take your company from just another Instagram account in the wild, to one that really flourishes online.

There's no reason for your company to not be on Instagram. At first, it seemed like more of a platform for users that had important photographs to share rather than products to sell. Now, it's clear that there is no better way to share your company's information than to get on Instagram. With the app being owned by Facebook, the two together can be immensely helpful in aiding your expansive business ventures.

What is Instagram?

Instagram is a social media platform in which users can share photographic posts with texts, hash-tags, location and people tags. You also have the ability to comment and like comments from followers.

A more recent addition to the platform is the use of Instagram stories, in which users can share posts for up to 24 hours, (which also includes the ability to save highlights of stories straight to your Instagram bio).

There is even Instagram TV (otherwise known as IGTV), where you can find both professionally produced and amateur self made video content. All of these tools offer a way for you to share content and market yourself to any number of Instagram users.

Instagram started with Kevin Systrom's desire to make sharing photographs beautiful and simple. Eventually, people started to invest in Kevin's ideas, and he soon quit his job and started up the app known as Burbn with Mike Krieger.

The two decided to stick to their goal of creating a new form of communication that would primarily use images. Eventually, the app grew to host millions of users, and was purchased by Facebook for a whopping 1 billion in 2012.

There were other apps that focused on sharing images at the time, like Photobucket or even Facebook. What set Instagram apart, however, was the quality of these photographs. Your image had to be a certain size, and you could only post one image at a time. There were filters built into the app as well that helped to really elevate these images. You could follow people, but that wouldn't mean that they would follow you back. This kind of high-quality app made people get on it at a rapid rate.

There are an estimated 800 million users on Instagram, and the number doesn't seem to be dropping any time soon. Five hundred million of these users check their Instagram every day, over 30 percent checking multiple times a day, on average. That's hundreds of millions of opportunities for users to see your brand or product.

What this means is that just because someone doesn't see your Instagram post the first time around doesn't mean it'll be ignored. Some 30 percent of your followers are going to get on the platform once or twice that day, which means your image can still get shown to them.

Kylie Jenner is a notable user of Instagram that managed to take her company, Kylie Cosmetics, to a 900 million estimated net worth, spending almost nothing on advertising. While she pays for photo-shoots of her products and all the marketing involved in the design, little to nothing was initially paid for sharing those ads, and instead, she was able to use her own social media profile to promote her products.

Her sisters, Kim Kardashian, and Khloe Kardashian followed soon after with their makeup and clothing companies. This is the new way to sell clothes and makeup, it seems. While that might not be your brand, you can still learn something from this highly successful business model. A lot of clothing used to be sold through paparazzi photographs of celebrities.

You might have seen Britney Spears walk into a Starbucks in a green tank top, only for that look to pop up in the trendiest stores soon after. The same thing is happening now, but at a rapid rate, and celebrities are doing it themselves. This kind of advertisement is revolutionary, and though many people won't reach the wealth status of Kylie Jenner, we can use her methods as inspiration for our own brands.

Interactive stories and using product placement with notable faces helps take your advertising from basic to innovative with the click of a few buttons. People will have the ability to look through your story and see tagged products if you are someone that owns an online store. All kinds of tags can help connect you with users to get your business to a place where it thrives.

Location tags can help connect your brand to places that others might be vacationing. Your followers can tag themselves at your restaurant when they visit, letting people see that they recommend your food. You can tag people in pictures as well so that you're connecting your page through theirs by their tagged images section. Hash-tagging your images is very important as well. Basically, tags offer a way for people to follow their favorite hobbies, and find communities they can relate to.

Chapter 7 - How to Use Instagram Organic Marketing to Grow Your Business or Brand

The greatest thing about using any social media platform is that you can start with nothing. It's a free app, and even if you don't have any followers, you can start to grow your audience within the hour.

Brands on Instagram get 30 percent more engagement from followers compared to brand profiles on Facebook. So it's clear to see that *The 'Gram* is where you're going to be making the most money if you're looking to sell consumer products.

Just like Facebook, you have to start with a strong brand. Instagram is more aesthetic based. You can check out anyone's Instagram profile and see that they might have a theme, whether it's through images or colors. Having a strong theme like this can help bring your brand to the next level. People will start to associate these easy images with your product and will better recognize one of your ads when it pops up into their feed.

Having a few people that already follow you will be very helpful in expanding your brand, but don't worry if you don't even have an Instagram already. This is where marketing yourself or your own page is really going to come in handy as well, as people like the authenticity of Instagram and how close they feel to the individuals that they follow. So if you have, say, a clothing store, don't limit yourself to just having a business page. People like to see the faces of those that they are giving their money to. It feels more "real" even if the interaction is through a highly popular social media app.

While Facebook's organic marketing is decreasing, Instagram's organic reach is still going strong. More people are willing to listen to individuals that they already follow, taking their advice to purchase a product or buy into an idea. And Instagram offers users an aesthetically pleasing way to view the things that they wish to spend their money on.

Your best option is to market yourself and create a strong brand that people want to follow. Let's say that your company is one that isn't automatically aesthetically pleasing, such as a service that helps people write resumes. This isn't a pretty product you can take a picture of, or a shirt that you can hire a model to wear. You also don't want to just put pictures of resumes on your Instagram, as that would be boring. This is where you will actually have to be more creative than if you were someone selling a physical product.

Your goal, in this instance, will be to create posts that are interactive and that educate people. For example, making a colorful Infographic on the statistics of the likelihood that someone will get hired based on a certain word in their cover letter is a great way to inform your followers with useful information. You could also make quick video tutorials on how to layout the header of a resume. Your company doesn't have to post full tutorials, but sharing free tidbits of information makes users feel like you're really in it to help them and not just to try to trick them into buying your services.

Instagram seems to be rapidly rising, but it isn't even ten years old yet! It's clear to see that this is one of the top choices for businesses looking to grow their following and generate business leads.

Start by making sure that you are following the right brands on Instagram. If, for example, you use your restaurants Instagram profile to follow Kim Kardashian, and all of her fashion-focused sisters, then you're not going to get very many engaged users interested in your food-related posts.

Instead, follow other restaurants in the area, and notable people that might frequent your eatery. Not only will you show up in front of a more niche-targeted audience, but you can also keep an eye on your competition to see what interests your customers.

Capturing Business Leads Has Never Been Easier

Getting business leads on Instagram is going to be just like how you would go about this process with the other forms of social media. You might first start by considering the creation of a landing page on your website. This would be a page that the user gets taken to directly from Instagram.

All Instagram account profiles can have a single link in their bio that your followers can click and then get taken over to your website. But be sure that where you send users is also relevant to your Instagram posts overall.

If users are taken straight to your site, but your website is not a place where they can get more information about whatever you've posted on your Instagram account, then they might feel slightly cheated.

For example, if you put a link on a photograph of a certain shirt on your website, but the user clicks the link and gets taken straight to the homepage of your website, they're going to get annoyed that they weren't taken directly to the original shirt.

Just like Facebook, people don't get on Instagram to shop right away. That might be what comes of their time on that platform, but the original intention was to look at pictures. If they have to jump through too many hoops to get what they want, then you're going to lose them. So, the easier you can make things for others, the more likely they will be to spend their money on your products. That is why it's important for you to give them a personal, individualized experience that will keep them coming back to you.

Running an Instagram contest can be a great way for people to start to get more interested in your company as well. People love entering contests, being interactive on social media, and entering the chance to get free stuff. By having them sign up for a newsletter, or even follow you on social media as an incentive, you are getting them to buy into your brand and company right off the bat.

Having posts that give you a chance to win $50 for following you will be a simple way to get more people to your page. Some might unfollow after the contest, but you have to expect that certain people will stay, giving you a chance to reach out to them with more sales opportunities later on.

Following people is a great free way to get traffic to your website as well. All you have to do is find the right potential clients and simply follow them. Or you can look at your competitors profiles to see who is following them, and follow those people too.

Now, whenever you follow a person there is a good chance that they'll check out your Instagram profile. If they like what they see, then they may follow you right back. If they don't like your posts, then they won't, but that's fine because you didn't spend any money on simply following them.

It's important, however, to keep use this following tactic sparingly. Companies that follow say over 2,000 people look spammy and come across like they are just following you to get a follow back.

While this might work for some people, you don't want it to be your main strategy. Start first by following your team, whether it's the top two people that founded the company, or the 20 employees at your restaurant. This is important so that others can see the social interactions among the workers, making it feel like a more authentic brand. After that, follow people in your area that seem to have an interest in your company. Try to not go over more than 500 followers, or else people will know that you're just following to get one back.

You don't want those kinds of followers either. It can distort your analytics to have your Instagram profile have some 1,000 followers, yet you're following 3,000 people. Those followers are not going to see your posts anyways. Instead, focus on gathering legitimate followers. People will be more likely to follow you back if they think that you chose to follow them personally.

Mix Instagram and your company together as much as possible. At the real-world location of your business, have something notable on display showing your Instagram profile. For example, some restaurants or bars might have an interesting wall mural or a big fancy couch that people like to sit on. Your business patrons will be more likely to share their experience with an interesting picture, and they can tag you in it.

One thing some people overlook when getting leads online are the followers they already have. Most brands are hungry for new followers, when really, they can still make a ton of money from the people that are already following them. So give your current followers freebie offers, discounts and other opportunities to get rewarded for their loyalty to your brand or business.

Turning Likes Into Website Traffic

In order to drive traffic to your website, you must first get a good number of people interacting with your posts. This doesn't always mean commenting and having conversations, but at least "liking" your pictures. When a user likes a post on your profile, all the people that they follow can also see that they liked your post.

So give people a reason to like your posts. Ask them a question or put a poll on your story that has people thinking about you and remembering that they interacted with you as well. The simple hashtag #linkinbio is popular for many different Instagram users to get their followers to not only go to their page to see more posts, but to click on a link that takes them directly to their site.

If you're selling a product, make sure that you actually have a business page on Instagram. This gives you the chance to have a button where your followers can actually send you a message right away.

Plus, having a business profile will also give you Insights in which you can view statistics such as the gender of your followers, their age range, what their location is, and how many hours they spend online.

This is very similar to Facebook, and gives you the opportunity to make more specific posts. We won't get into the specifics of what the best thing to post is, because we already talked a lot about that in the last section. The same kind of thing goes for Instagram. People like looking at pictures of other people, and clear, easy to understand images and posts are going to be the most successful.

Transform High Engagement Into Sales And Revenue

The number one way to generate product sales is to first get people to your products website page. But we also have to remind ourselves that our customers do not naturally want to visit our website. If they could, they would prefer to simply click "like" on an image and have that product delivered to their doorstep. It is your responsibility, then, to give them an easy way to sign up for your services or products instead.

So don't make them jump through hoops to get to the spending money part, or else they will give up and go away. There are so many different companies out there vying for our customers attention. So we have to be very appreciative of fact that our customers choose to leave their Instagram feed just to come visit our website.

Now, when it comes to Facebook for example, you don't want to be too pushy because it's an app where users primarily look to interact with their families and friends. The same can be said about Instagram, but even more so. People will scroll through ten pictures, and if they see that 5 of them are ads, they are going to get annoyed and start unfollowing.

Give your followers interesting and aesthetically pleasing pictures that they will be happy to "like." The more likes and activity you get on your post, the higher a chance it will pop up in the "explore" page of other individuals that don't even follow you.

Instagram's explore page is a great way for you to get your Instagram posts in front of individuals that don't currently follow you. The things that show up on any given explore page will include people's images that they might have looked up, the images their friends like, and images based off the people they follow and the things they like.

Don't look at your Instagram posts as ads, whether they're sponsored or not. This is how many top celebrities and influencer's find so much success. They integrate their products into their daily life like they would anything else. There are formulas for commercials and advertisements that work, but Instagram is different. You want to make your followers feel like they know you and that you are a friend giving a recommendation, not a company trying to sell a product.

Not only will people be less likely to avoid your product out of spite, or the fact that they don't want to give into an advertisement, but they will actually feel like buying the product is *their* idea.

Instagram stories are great ways to get people excited as well, because they are more common, and you can post more frequently. Not only can you share your own posts, but you can start to share what others are posting about you as well. For example, if someone creates an Instagram or story post about the beauty product their using from your company, you can share that post straight to your story, letting others see how much they like your product.

Chapter 8 - How to Use Instagram Paid Marketing to Grow Your Business or Brand

Now that you're aware of the free and organic ways that you can market your brand, it's time to get into the ways that you can start spending your money to get some serious return on your marketing investments.

There are two important avenues that you can use for your paid marketing Instagram efforts: paid ads and paid sponsorships.

Sponsorships will involve partnering with an influencer, or another brand, in order to get your products in the hands of users. Popular products that are often seen with influencer's include makeup brands and health supplements such as Sugar Bear Hair gummies. Clothing brands and monthly box subscriptions are also very popular paid sponsorships.

Sponsorships work so well because there is a trust created between a brand and a consumer. Anyone can turn on the TV right now and watch an ad with someone giving a testimonial. Usually, in the corner, in small, white print, there might be a disclaimer that the situations are dramatizations or that they are paid actors. This automatically makes you not trust the brand. Not only are they blatantly trying to get you to buy their products, but they also lied to you, making us question if they are doing this because they can't find anyone that will actually support their testimonials.

Remember when we talked about how Kylie Jenner can make a million dollars for one post? Well, we can assume that you don't have that kind of money, and if you do, you seem to have it figured out already! What you can start with, however, if you don't have much money, is a collaboration that mutually benefits two different parties. If you sell dresses, maybe you want to partner with a company that sells shoes. The two of you can post the same picture of a model wearing the shoes and the hat, and the followers you each have will cross over, exposing your product or service to a completely new audience.

Don't expect to go to someone with a million followers right away and offer a few hundred dollars for one post. Start smaller, with so-called *micro-influencer's*. People will be much more likely to trust someone with fewer followers rather than a person like Kim Kardashian, who has over a hundred million followers.

Instead, you might want to find a person with only 5,000 followers, offering them $100 and a free sample of one of your products. Though you're only reaching 5,000 followers, a lot more of those followers are going to trust the micro-influencer's recommendation.

Determining how much you pay for a post is going to be up to you. If you are selling clothing in the $20-$50 range, you might still charge the same as you would for a $2 app download. This is because you are more likely to persuade the micro-influencer's followers to download your low-cost app, whereas only 20 people might buy one of your higher-priced clothing products.

Now, picking the right person to sponsor your product is also going to be very important. You'll want to first look at their overall aesthetic and ask if it is in line with your brand. Then, look at their followers and check the quality of them and the kind of interactions they have. Be wary of influencer's who have purchased their followers and likes.

One important thing to remember is the FTC's limitations on what can be shared with sponsors. The most important thing to remember is that the followers of that influencer have a right to know when that person is being paid to promote your product. Rather than the influencer blatantly stating, "I'm being paid for this," they might instead discuss how they've started a partnership, or they are trying out a new company.

Make The Instagram Feed Your Own Personal Cash-cow

The most important thing you are going to get from your Instagram ads includes business leads, website traffic, and product sales. Many of the same rules for using Facebook ads will apply to how you're going to use Instagram ads. It's up to you to determine if your brand should be selling things through videos or pictures. Study important marketing strategies for creating organic pictures and try out new methods to see what your followers will interact with the most.

What differs from Facebook, is the use of stories and how popular these have become for many Instagram users. Not only can you organically use your own stories to advertise to your followers already, but ads play in between these stories, and you can purchase your own spot.

Sometimes, people won't even notice that they are looking at an ad, and that's going to be very helpful when creating your own ad posts. Try to create ad posts that look authentic and natural to the overall feel of Instagram. That means creating ad posts that wouldn't look out of place on any half-decent Instagram feed, such as posts that use bright colors, engaging imagery, bold subtitles and the like.

Next, the process of selecting viewers and creating shareable content will be the same as making a regular sponsored post on Instagram. Just make sure that you are selecting story mode and that you've created a vertical image that fits in with the style of other story ads on Instagram.

Once you start using Instagram story ads, it's time to understand the importance of keeping the attention of Instagram users (and preventing the dreaded 'Swipe-Through').

Some business minds think the key to getting people to buy into their products is to bombard them with information or to try and do the hard-sell.

But getting someone's attention isn't going to the be way that you get them to buy your product, however. You might have the money to buy up all the ad spots, but that doesn't mean you should do that right away. Instead, start integrating normal and non-offensive ads into people's Instagram stories, and they'll appreciate your product much more.

Having to look at an ad can feel intrusive enough when watching Instagram stories, so try not to make your ad feel too 'pushy'. Let it become something that they would look at anyway. The first few seconds of your story are the most important seconds in the entire process. Most Instagram stories are viewed with the sound on, so using a nice tune that isn't overly annoying can be helpful.

The best kinds of ads, however, are visual ones that will stick in the user's mind, but don't use a branded image or logo if you're brand or business isn't quite established yet. People simply won't recognize your logo, so don't start with that approach right away.

Instead, create general and relatable images that draw new users in and raise interest in those that don't know as much about you just yet.

Chapter 9 - The Power of Youtube (And How To Use It To Grow Your Business or Brand)

The first video to ever be loaded to Youtube was "Me at the Zoo," that featured Jawed Karim at the San Diego Zoo, April 23, 2005. Within a year and a half, Google purchased the company for $1.65 billion dollars.

Over a billion Youtube users log in every single month, and all of those people are potential viewers for your advertisements.

And aside from Google, Youtube is one of the most used search engines online. It's pretty wild to think that there are almost as many people looking things up on Youtube as they are on Google.

Youtube is almost like TV now, with more users and young adults watching Youtube in place of regular cable. What's particularly beneficial for businesses is the fact that people are also more accepting of Youtube advertisements.

If you're going to watch a 10-minute Youtube video, you've come to accept that there will be a 30 second advertisement shown at the start of the video. This has caused Youtube users to become conditioned to accept watching Youtube commercials just like they're conditioned to watch TV commercials.

Your company can benefit from having a Youtube channel that shares videos and instructional clips that help expose people to your brand. You can make money from the ads shown on your Youtube videos, as well as advertising your own products and services.

In other words, Youtube allows you to present your products 'in-action' and show-off their effectiveness in real-time, whilst also allowing you to make a nice side income from the other ads that play during your video.

For example, if you have run a gym you can use Youtube to show workout tutorials or give instructions on how to make healthy nutritious meals.

Though you might not have originally thought of creating a Youtube channel, it can be a great way to market your business while simultaneously making you even more money outisde of your current business income.

What's great about this platform is that very few small businesses are even on Youtube; in fact, it's estimated that only 9 percent of small businesses have a Youtube Channel.

But the fact remains that Youtube is the world's second largest search engine. This means that it is integrated into our society and won't be going anywhere anytime soon. The videos that you create today will also stay relevant and active in people's Youtube recommended video feeds.

Compare Youtube's long-lived content to Instagram's feed, for example. You'll rarely see a post on Instagram from a few years ago, and more often than not, old posts are left dormant and buried - lost in the annals of Instagram time.

Whilst on Youtube, sure, you could post a video and that video may get 10,000 views in a week leaving you feeling ecstatic at its success. But think about the incredible long-term potential that video has over the next decade, and the likelihood it has to collect more and more views over time!

What is Youtube, really?

Youtube has over a billion users that log in every month. That alone is a massive number and doesn't even account for those that don't have accounts. Who hasn't watched a Youtube video without actually logging into their Youtube account?

But with Youtube, however, there are many videos people will repeatedly watch (and will watch again in the future).

Sixty percent of Youtube users say they prefer watching videos online to watching TV live via their cable subscription. In fact, one of the biggest indicators of Youtube staking a real claim to its place in television broadcasting was when Youtube hosted a presidential debate in 2012.

But founding Youtube wasn't easy, but it was quick and got popular fast because it was a site that needed to exist. Now, there are countless video sharing apps and many more in the works, yet Youtube has continued to dominate the online video viewing world.

Not being on Youtube would be a disservice to your brand. It's safe to say that Youtube has very few equals in terms of overall product, and not many threatening competitors. A new app would have to offer a lot of incentive for users to switch, so getting on Youtube now is crucial to joining on the ever-changing innovations of media sharing.

Some three hundred hours worth of video content get uploaded to Youtube every 60 seconds, so it's important that you create content that can truly stand out from the rest. Which means that whatever video content you choose create, whether it's an ad or not, it needs to be something that provide Youtube viewers with value.

There are lots of different factors that go into creating video content; in fact I recommend that you check out *Social Media Marketing Content*

Creation Guide' written by Aron Bordelon for all the best tips and advice on creating engaging Youtube videos. But in this book, we're only going to focus on how to <u>market</u> your business or brand on Youtube.

Chapter 10 - How to Use Youtube Organic Marketing to Grow Your Business or Brand

You could take a video, and have it uploaded and watched by 100 people by the end of the day. Writing a script, shooting and editing a film, and distributing it takes years, but we can have a video of our cat licking itself available for billions to see with very little effort.

Because of this accessibility, there is a lot to sift through on the Internet. That is why it can be so important for us to brand ourselves properly. When you can take a unique idea and ride with it, you will get a company that people love and one that will be around for years to come. The most successful brands are ones that are leaders. They consist of people that are thinking of new ideas and finding ways to solve problems we didn't even realize existed.

Now, we won't go into detail about how to actually create a brand new Youtube channel, because Youtube have created a platform that will guide you through the whole process of getting started. Its called 'Youtube Creators' and can be found at *https://CreatorAcademy.Youtube.com.*

It's free, user-friendly and makes creating a new Youtube account straightforward.

Instead, this chapter is going to go over organic Youtube marketing, which means using the free tools the channel provides to get your brands and products out for customers to see and purchase.

The best way to start your Youtube marketing efforts is to first think of an overall theme for your channel. You don't have to post the same type of video over and over and over again, but you do have to have a general theme for the content you're going to post. If you're a freelance writer, for example, then you should have writing-related videos. Adding in random videos about PC games may leave your Youtube subscribers feeling confused. Instead, focus on one niche, one idea that you're going to share with others and how you're going to do that.

Your goal is to get people watching, viewing, liking, sharing, and subscribing to your content just as you would want on Instagram and Facebook. All of these social media platforms are similar, but your methods of finding, getting, and keeping your Youtube audience differs slightly.

But note that even though your Youtube channels content might be different than what's posted on your Instagram profile, at the end of the day, your brand should still be clear and consistent - regardless of the fact that they are being shown on opposing platforms.

However, try not to fall into the trap of simply filling your Youtube channel with videos that are little more than an endless stream of adverts for your products. While that's completely fine on one hand, on the other, getting users to like and subscribe to you will require a more interactive strategy.

For example, if you own a restaurant, consider creating how-to tutorials on seasonal recipes that could get viewers really interested in visiting your eatery. Or lets say that you are an aspiring beauty guru, you could decide to record makeup tutorials, the exact sort of content that can attract a large audience on Youtube.

Furthermore, someone looking to create a personal brand might place more of an emphasis on vlogging and connect with their audience by sharing a glimpse into their day-to-day life.

Snag The Attention Of The Casual Viewer

With so much video content freely available on Youtube, it's important that you focus your energy on creating video content that is instantly clickable and offers your audience something that will entice them watch your video.

Sticking to a weekly video posting schedule is also important, but it's up to you to decide what the right frequency is for your brand and your product.

Some people find that they need to post every single day to stay relevant, while other individuals might only need to post once a week. Either way, you have to be consistent. Posting once every month can cause people to forget about you. Start by posting at least once a week. If you're not getting a ton of views, post more frequently. And listen and interact with your viewers to see which parts of your content aren't working and which parts are chiming with your audience.

After you've figured out what your video is going to consist of, you have to ensure that you have a clickable thumbnail and eye-catching title. The title will be important because it's going to be what causes your video to show up in any given search engine. Use a strong, bold title to draw people in, and then follow it with a shorter subtitle to explain the video further.

Next, you're going to want to make sure that your thumbnail is eye-catching. You might find that your title is the same as the video someone else has, but the thumbnail could be what sets you apart. It should include an image that's in the video, first and foremost. Videos that include random unrelated pictures as a form of image click-bait might do well in grabbing some early video views, but they will eventually get thumbed down, and people won't watch as often.

Second, include another title, or at least a keyword in the picture as well. Using red arrows and circling things can be helpful. Sometimes, things might be very obvious in a picture, but using a circle is what helps draw people's eyes towards your video so they can decide to click and watch.

Your best Youtube "business leads" will be the people who actually take the time to subscribe to your channel. People can watch your videos whenever they want, (as long as you don't have your video listed as 'private'), so they can view your videos without having to subscribe to your channel.

This is why it's important to give Youtube viewers a strong reason to subscribe to you. Ask yourself, *what are you going to do to get people wanting more?*

How To Get Your Subscribers To Keep Coming Back For More

Putting out regular video content is going to be an important part of growing your Youtube channel. Youtube users are always hungry for new content, but they equally crave the consistency from their favorite video channels.

Just as with traditional serialized TV cable shows, we have to remember that Youtube viewers also want to follow Youtube channels that can be relied upon for regular new content.

Tagging your video is a great way to help people find your videos. You can add these tags to the videos description and in the videos tagging sidebar. Your videos description can be quite long, too, and it is a great place to tell your audience a little bit about your business. You also have the opportunity (within the video description) to link viewers to your website or to encourage them to subscribe to your channel.

Your video description, however, isn't the first thing people see on your video (obviously, since they will be watching your video first and foremost).

For example, on Facebook, what your Facebook posts caption text is typically the thing that captures people's attention. But when it comes to Youtube, you might find that a lot of people don't even read your description.

Another thing you need to keep in mind is your videos 'search-ability' (otherwise known as Youtube SEO - Search Engine Optimization).

Use Youtube to search for your own video by typing in keywords and phrases that relate to your video's content. If your video doesn't pop up, look at the most popular videos in the search results and note down what they've put in their video title, descriptions and video tags. You can begin using similar tags to help rank your own videos in Youtube's search results.

It's important to know that tagging the most popular things aren't going to get you views. While you might assume that adding a #kyliejenner or #donaldtrump tag to your video will get views, it will only make people annoyed that they clicked your video and didn't get what they were looking for. Don't try to trick people into clicking on your video. While it might work for some, it can end up causing people to dislike your videos or even report them.

Using captioned videos can be very beneficial as well, especially if you're making an instructional video or a blog. There aren't as many captioned videos available for people that can't hear, or those that don't want to watch with the volume off, so this alone allows you to get more views. You'll also find that it helps your SEO optimization because your captions become their own descriptions and tags that could lead searchers to your videos.

Give people a reason to comment on your video. If you watch any blogger or person that often posts and makes money on Youtube, they'll tell you at some point in the video, verbally or textually, to share a comment. This is because it helps drive traffic to your videos which will ultimately drive traffic to your website. Ask them to comment with their opinion, or what they didn't like about the video. Ask them if there's something they want to see, or if they don't like what you're doing, and you should do something else. Whatever they say will not only be helpful in improving your brand, but you will also find that it draws more attention to your channel.

Reach Out To Other Youtube Channels

Just like with Instagram, you can team up with Youtube influencer's to sell your products on their channels. Now, while this can be helpful, it can also be something that ends up costing you a fair amount of money.

So in order to drive product sales using free organic Youtube marketing, a great way to get word of mouth out there is by getting Youtubers to review your products.

Try sending your product to Youtube influencer's for free. In exchange, they will record and post an honest review about your product on their channel. Their followers will trust the opinion of the Youtube influencer, and so will be more open and willing to buy your product.

Product sales can also come about as a result of your within your own videos. You can demonstrate how to use the product or do a review of it. Showing people testing your products can be a fun way to get more involved as well.

Chapter 11 - How to Use Youtube Paid Marketing to Grow Your Business or Brand

While Youtube has many great free features that help users connect with their customers and advertise their products, it's also important to understand the benefits of all the options for paid ads.

You don't even have to have a Youtube account at all if it seems completely irrelevant to your company. Instead, you can use Youtube's Display ads. These are ads that will be displayed right above the other suggested videos on the right side of your web browser screen. They will be the first thing that many people see when the video they selected is open.

Display ads might also appear within the videos in the form of *cards* or overlay ads at the bottom of the video. These are all classic ad types and can be very beneficial for your brand.

There are some important things to understand about these simple types of "display ads," however. First, they are usually not exciting, consisting of text and simple images. If you do choose to use a display ad, you have to make sure that you build a sense of interest from your audience.

Sometimes, people think the best way to build a sense of interest is to shove as much information they can in one post. You don't always have to do this, however. Instead, you can build interest and get people intrigued by what it is you might be leading them to.

Many people also have the ability to simply block these kinds of ads out. Can you remember the last commercial you saw? Maybe. Can you remember the last display ad you saw on the side of your screen or in the video? Not as likely.

Your best option is going to be video ads, and that's what we'll be covering in the last section of this part.

Leverage The Power Of Youtube Video Ads

The most important thing you are going to get from your Youtube ads includes business leads, website traffic, and product sales. You can make money from simple Youtube views and other sponsorships. The most money, however, is going to come from people that go to your website and buy your product. When you add up the revenue from views and clicks on your videos, each user might only give less than a penny towards your video profit. If they make it to your site, however, they might end up spending over $50 on your products.

The most common form of Youtube ads includes TrueView ads. These are the short 5 to 20 second long videos that play before a video starts playing.

These videos require viewers to watch for a few seconds, even though the ad itself may be a couple minutes long. The viewer then has the option to skip the ad, though they might end up watching the entire thing. These ads are very important for you to understand, as they are one of <u>the most effective</u> Youtube ad product available to you right now.

Longer ads are obviously more effective than shorter ones on an individual user basis. It's easier to convince someone to do something within 3 minutes than it is if you are only given ten seconds. However, your longer ads won't be as available to the same amount of people that the shorter ads are.

So it's important to have a strong ad that lasts a few seconds and can be played on its own while having a longer version of that ad that can play afterward. Changing up the type of ads you have and how long they might be, is going to be your best Youtube ad strategy approach.

Bumper ads are adverts that only last 6 seconds or last and they are not skippable. There is also not an option to watch the entire ad. If you've ever watched a video on Youtube before, then you've probably already experienced watching one of these types of adverts. They are sort of our payment for watching the video in the first place. You have to remember that these videos are likely going to be ignored, so yours really has to stand out.

The most important thing to remember with your ad is that you have to give people a reason not to watch the video that they've selected. They've already made up their mind, so what is it about your product that's going to change it?

A lot of people might see your product, think to themselves that they like it, and then envision themselves going back later and looking more into the product. By the time they've finished the video, however, they've forgotten about your product and have moved onto the next video. If you can't get them to stop what they're doing and leave the video, then you have to at least give them an ad that they're going to remember.

Chapter 12 – The Power of LinkedIn (And How To Use It To Grow Your Business or Brand)

LinkedIn is a little different from other social media sites. The original intention wasn't for this to be a place where friends and family could connect, but rather, it was a place for those who were looking for work and those companies looking to hire them.

It was founded in 2002, and after just six short years, it became a company valued at nearly 1 billion dollars. Reid Hoffman, the creator of LinkedIn, knew that it was important for people to have a place online where they could connect, rather than depend on corporate meet-ups and conferences for networking opportunities.

Reid Hoffman originally planned on becoming a philosopher, following more of an academic career pathway in life. But over time, he soon decided to turn his attention towards the expanding online world of the 90s and pursued his dream of building a software company.

While studying at Stanford, Reid wanted to look for a way that he could reach more people, realizing the power he could have with software that extends to minds ready to be influenced. Though LinkedIn wasn't originally created for connecting with friends - like Facebook or Instagram - Reid began his entrepreneurial foray into the online social media sphere first by creating an app called *Socialnet*. The app was designed to provide a way for people to online date — as well as connect with other small business owners.

This wasn't working out the way that Reid planned, but luckily, he had a friend that connected him to Max Levchin, who eventually went on to develop PayPal with Peter Thiel.

After working for an online business startup - that quickly becoming successful in its own right - Reid made enough money to invest in his own company, LinkedIn. It started with just 13 people, who invited about 112 people to join. Reid was like many other software developers that just had to wait and see if they had what it took to really take off. And today, now that LinkedIn has over 500 million members, it's clear that Reid knew exactly what he was doing, finding success like many of the others that we've already discussed throughout the book.

LinkedIn isn't about getting liked or sharing funny cat videos. Instead, it's a straight-to-the-point service that provides you the direct opportunity to market yourself. There's no hiding that you're trying to make money once you put yourself on LinkedIn. There won't be a hidden #ad in the comment section, and you won't be trying to convince followers to buy into your product with influencer marketing. Instead, you are given the tools needed to brand yourself and connect with other individuals that need or want your products and services.

LinkedIn is most important for those that are interested in B2B marketing. B2B is in reference to *business-to-business*, which deals with those companies that are looking to market their products and services towards other businesses, rather than selling on an individual, consumer level.

LinkedIn is going to be a bit easier for its users as well. There isn't a need to alleviate the social media barrier between searching for entertainment and getting something sold to you. People are on LinkedIn for the reason that you're on there as well. While it might be easier in that sense to market yourself on LinkedIn versus other social media, it's also important to remember that this means a lot more competition.

Why Should YOU Care About LinkedIn?

LinkedIn is a place where Fortune 500 owners and recruitment staff go to search for new talent, prospects, projects, and people to join their team and help expand their businesses.

We've already highlighted how many users are on LinkedIn, and with that number, you might feel initial skepticism. Many users will make a LinkedIn account, only to abandon it when they find a different job. Still, at least 40 percent of users get on LinkedIn on a daily basis, which means that there are at least 100 million people you still have access to.

Whether you're looking to market your company or simply share your brand, LinkedIn is still very important and relevant to the business world and those that wish to make money.

While it's clear to see that LinkedIn is still very culturally relevant, the hope for the company, as stated by Jeff Weiner, is to get LinkedIn to a multi-billion user number, and have it be the largest job posting site and home of working professionals not just on this continent, but in the entire world.

It's clear that this company isn't going away anytime soon. Particularly as out of their hundreds of millions of users, there are over 50 million senior-level influencer's on the platform, with some 40 million important decision-making executives on board as well.

So LinkedIn is more than simply a place for individuals to find work. It is a place where important influencer's are actively investing their money, and it's high time for you to cash in on some of that investment!

Earlier in this book, we stated that Google bought Youtube for over a billion dollars, and that it an incredible price-tag for a single business acquisition. But it pales in comparison to the $25 billion that Microsoft purchased LinkedIn for!

What's more, LinkedIn isn't just for older, more established users either. There are at least 87 million millennials on LinkedIn, and these are the people that are going to be making major decisions in the coming decades. Out of all the social media sites we've discussed so far, LinkedIn should be the number one choice for those that are in B2B marketing. This is because 94 percent of B2B marketers are already on LinkedIn! Don't be the 6 percent that misses out on this lucrative opportunity.

Chapter 13 - How to Use LinkedIn Paid Marketing to Grow Your Business or Brand

If you have a B2B company and are not on LinkedIn, it's safe to say that at the moment, you are actually losing business. Don't get too scared right away, because luckily, we have ways of organic marketing on LinkedIn that you can use to make money for your company.

LinkedIn is more niche than other social media platforms, depending on your business, but it is less complicated to use when it comes to finding leads, clients, and customers. However first, let's look at a few of the mistakes that people make, and the challenges that LinkedIn presents to users seeking to profitably leverage its platform.

LinkedIn is pretty much a small social media platform compared to the behemoths that are Facebook, Youtube, or Instagram. With the amount of traffic a larger platform - such as Instagram - receives everyday, you could sit on Instagram all day and like pictures, read posts, watch videos, and pretty much never run out of new content to see and interact with.

On LinkedIn, however, there is a clear motive behind interactions on the platform, and its users are more purposeful in what they're looking for. This is useful for you to keep in mind when going about formulating your LinkedIn marketing strategy. You need to try and bear in mind that LinkedIn is not purely about posting interesting entertaining content. Rather, you content needs to give LinkedIn users unique and actionable information that's specific to their needs.

A big mistake that LinkedIn users make is thinking that this app isn't where they will find success. Some people get on and see that the site isn't working for them, so they take their business elsewhere and give up on that site, putting an emphasis on Facebook or Instagram. This is where the mistake is made. It's not the app that isn't working, but what you're putting on the app that might not be giving you the results that you are hoping for.

Navigating the app and having accessibility to the clients you need will never be the problem. The biggest challenge you will face on LinkedIn is getting your content viewed. The biggest mistake that you could make is thinking that your content is fine and that it's the app that's the issue. When something isn't working, it's important to try something new rather than hoping that a different site will provide you with the results you want.

The next two sections are going to highlight the two most important things to do with organic marketing on LinkedIn: *1). Posting Quality Content and, 2). Posting Frequency.*

It's The Post Quality, Stupid

The thing that is most important for your LinkedIn profile is for you to make sure the account always posting quality content.

This doesn't mean posting a picture on there that can be "liked," or having an article that more people are likely to click on. You have to make sure that your content is also very shareable. Reaching out to the people that already follow you is important, and you can't overlook those that you already connect with. If you do this, then you aren't creating a great business where clients can depend on you.

What you also have to do, however, is ensure that you're not overlooking those individuals that you might have the ability to reach out to. Each person you're in contact with has a few others that might benefit from knowing about your business, so having ten followers could mean that you have the potential to reach out to twenty or more individuals if each one of your followers share your post with just one other person.

You can see how quickly creating something viral can be important in ensuring that your content is shown to the various users on Linked. In fact, most of the top content that you'll see at any given time will be things that were specifically designed to be viral in the first place.

Your content needs to be very specific and lay out what it is that you are selling. It shouldn't be like Instagram and Facebook where you secretly hide a sale within an actual social media message. Instead, you should aim to have content that shows who you are, what you're selling, and what your mission is.

If you post vacation pictures, it will seem out of place, and people won't be interested in the content that you're sharing. Still, your content should be unique. Infographic's that offer new information and ideas that people haven't thought of before do the best on LinkedIn.

You could share statistics relating to your business niche, whilst explaining how your product or service can help to resolve any problems your followers or audience may have.

Engage with the audience and give them a reason to like or comment on your post. Most important, present something that other people want to have on their LinkedIn feed. If you give people interesting content that shares something new, (and looks good to boot), then you're going to have people sharing the image to their own feed, exposing your posts to even more potential clients.

Post Quality Is In The Eyes Of The Beholder

The importance of getting these business leads in the first place is to drive website traffic and increase your overall product sales. There are two more steps that you can take for organic LinkedIn marketing that can help you go from a profile that gets lost among the others to one that has active users engaging in your content.

The two key steps are to post frequently and be automated. This doesn't mean that you should start liking and commenting on everyone else's posts right away either. What you need to do first is ensure that you are putting out your own content that other people are most interested in interacting with.

Automated posts are ones that you can schedule at times of high traffic based on your personal analytics. You might have to use your own automated posting service if LinkedIn doesn't offer that on their own site just yet, but for now just know that it is very important that you post consistently and regularly.

Plus, by automating your LinkedIn posts, you save a tonne of time, and free yourself from having to worry about when to post what - and at what exact time.

But, don't make your profile too automated either. Sometimes, posting from your personal LinkedIn profile pages - as opposed to only posting from company official page - can turn out to be the edge you need to stand out from your competition.

You should be posting multiple times a day and aim to do so every few hours. This is why it's very helpful to use an automated service so that you can make sure you never miss a beat.

And don't be afraid to repost your content. Rather than coming up with three new pieces of content a day, maybe try reposting the same five posts throughout the week. This gives your posts a chance to be seen, especially as new posts get more attention, (even if its a reposted image or other piece of content).

Fun Fact: It is estimated that LinkedIn makes up 46 percent all in-bound social media traffic. In other words, this means that 4 out of 10 people that view your Youtube, Instagram, or Facebook content, may have come directly from your LinkedIn page. So even if you aren't using paid advertising methods on LinkedIn, it's still clear to see that organic marketing on LinkedIn can still help you grow your social media profile in other ways.

Chapter 14 - How to Use LinkedIn Paid Marketing to Grow Your Business or Brand

When you're putting your own money towards marketing, your goal is to obviously turn every ad click into a sale, client or follower of your brand. And in order for your ad investment to pay off, you have to make sure that your content is two things: relevant and consumable.

Relevancy is important because you need to create something that actually matters to the people that see your posts post. If your content doesn't apply to them, they will just keep scrolling.

Consumable content, on the other hand, means that the content is something that people can both understand and process with little effort. In other words, you don't want post 10-minute-long video ads as they require way too much time investment from an audience that has only just been introduced to your brand for the first time.

Now brand awareness is very important for all companies on social media platforms, and LinkedIn is no exception. You see, on LinkedIn, everyone is a professional that knows the importance of putting consistent content out there. That is why it's going to be crucial that you put out content that's relevant and shareable. But once you've created your content, distributing it to your audience is the next hurdle.

Using LinkedIn Paid Features

LinkedIn has a couple of paid features that are going to make it incredibly easy for you to reach out to other LinkedIn users;

InMail:

This paid features lets you access LinkedIn users personally for just $79 per month. Whilst that price may sound a little steep, you need to bear in mind that the response rate for InMail messages is three times that of regular direct messages.

This means that you can communicate with clients and leads directly into their inbox. So although a downside to InMail is the fact that you have to pay for it, once you start generating profitable business leads using this feature, you'll soon realize that it pays for itself.

Sales Solutions:

With this feature you can target new prospects with specific research, and then engage with them based upon that research. LinkedIn claims that this feature helps their users close more business deals and clients than ever before. This fact alone makes Sales Solutions a brilliantly useful tool for you to use!

Plus, anything that's going to help you make more money, in the end, is something that's very much going to be worth it. Having this kind of research at your fingertips allows you to see what works and what doesn't with your various marketing efforts on LinkedIn. It's important we look at this type of information so that we don't waste any of our time or resources that could better be used elsewhere.

Using LinkedIn Paid Ads

It's crucial that you start small with LinkedIn ads, because out of all the different social media paid ads described in this book, LinkedIn Ads are among the priciest.

So consider running your initial ad campaigns for just a few dollars a day to begin with. If you go too big at first, you might think that you're blasting your audiences, but instead, you might end up missing the mark and wasting away your hard-earned money. Money that could go towards a successful campaign that ends up tripling your sales.

Remember what we talked about in the last chapter. It's not LinkedIn that's the problem. If an ad isn't working, it's likely the content. By this point, however, you should be aware of the content that is going to do the best on LinkedIn.

The basic steps to actually start a campaign on LinkedIn is to create an account and decide what type of ad it is that you want. A lot of this is self-explanatory and very user-friendly on LinkedIn's site, so we won't go into the exact details of how to do that. Instead, let's look at the types of ads and which ones end up doing the best.

Sponsored posts are a great way to start. This will involve taking the posts that you already have on your LinkedIn page and paying extra to have them reach other viewers that aren't already following your LinkedIn profile.

These sponsored posts typically end up on the homepage of many LinkedIn users, providing them with an insight into what your company, business, service or brand is about.

You might not make huge sales from sponsored posts because people will just be getting to know you. What sponsored posts are good for, however, is getting you more followers, making people more aware of your brand, and increasing interest in your products and services.

Text ads are another great way to help people become more aware of your brand and increase traffic to your website. These are ads that will be dependent on headlines and descriptions. What's great about these types of ads is that you can experiment with headlines and ad copy, tweaking the ad until you find something that works best for you.

Chapter 15 - Conclusion

Anyone can see that social media plays a powerful role in our society today. While it seemed as just a past time when it first emerged, it is becoming a way of life and even a career for many. There are many important things to remember as a person that's involved with social media marketing. The three most important things we've learned in this book are that you need to have something valuable and worth selling, content that informs and entertains others, and a unique brand that keeps you standing out from the rest.

Your content should always provide value to your followers. One good way to look at this is to see what others are posting that gets a lot of attention. The things that the most popular sites are posting are definitely worth checking out so you can have an idea of what works best. At the same time, you have to make sure that your content is still unique. If you are only creating things that others have already put out there, then there's nothing that makes you stand out. Look for ways that you can twist things so they are new and fresh. Your content will have the most value when it can inform your followers, while entertaining them at the same time. This can be tricky to do, but once it's happened, you'll realize how many followers you can really get from this simple method.

Finally, you have to make sure that you've branded yourself. When you can come up with a clear vision for your business that shows in more way than one, then it will help your product stick out to viewers more, and they will remember your brand. When you are able to achieve those things, you will feel confident in your brand in the results will start to come in quickly.

Social media marketing is very powerful in our society. It plays a role in our online experience every time we open our phones. It can be challenging to escape the ubiquitous Facebook, Twitter, Instagram, and Youtube logos on products we buy and places that we go. And whilst trying to navigate social media can seem overwhelming, it is entirely possible for anyone to jump on board, especially those that want to market their brand or business on social media.

In the introduction, we discussed the different kinds of readers that have selected this book and all the benefits of what you will get after reading. There are many choices, but with the knowledge we provided and tips, you should be feeling confident about your ability to find success online.

Social media is so important to get on now because it is a free tool that can help take our business to the next level. You can pay to have your things marketed on social media, but you also should feel confident knowing you can get a great following from free marketing as well. There's a psychology behind social media, and that can be very beneficial to those that are hoping to navigate the online world of marketing.

In part 2, we covered the ways that you could use Facebook to grow your following and increase traffic to your page. With Facebook, one important thing to remember we covered is to not put encouragements to "like" or "share" posts, because the algorithms might filter this out of certain people's news feeds. You also want to make sure that you are posting content that is shareable. You can reach a lot of people through the pages of your followers if they decide to share your content. Most importantly, remember that you should use low-friction conversions. Anything that will require too much from your followers will end up making it harder for them to want to keep in contact and get leads from your business. You'll want to instead ensure that you are making things as easy as possible for new users.

Instagram is becoming just as powerful as Facebook once was. There is a lot of power with the types of marketing that you can choose to do on Instagram. You can join up with other Instagram accounts and have sponsored posts, or you can use run stories ads. Instagram is important to have because who you follow can play a crucial role in how much activity you get as well. If you follow similar accounts and people that are going to be most likely to follow you back, then you can grow your activity and end up finding that a lot of people will make their way to your website after having an initial interest. Remember the power of tagging when using Instagram as well. You'll want to tag people in pictures, tag locations, and use hash-tags to get extra activity to your page that wasn't going to get there initially. All of this is done organically as well, so it's inspiring to remember that we don't have to spend all of our money on marketing.

Youtube is such a powerful website that we wouldn't have expected to be so influential now. It's easy to see the popularity of watching videos online, but Youtube provides entire mini-series and even movies for their viewers. Anyone can create content and put in on Youtube, exposing it to millions of daily watchers. When marketing on Youtube, it's going to be important that you have a meaningful purpose. Perhaps you decide to have tutorials to show different kinds of ways to do things that relate to your business. You can also feel confident knowing that your content is likely going to show up in Youtube's recommended video feeds for years to come.

Finally, LinkedIn is an incredibly important platform right now for marketers and B2B businesses, because it is a website specifically designed for professionals. It's there for people looking to connect with other businesses, who might also be seeking to collaborate with like-minded entrepreneurs. Your competitive edge on this platform comes in the form of making sure that your content is distinctive and unique.

Throughout this book, we've given you the tools you need to get started on crafting your own successful social media marketing strategy. And right now, you have the unique opportunity to get ahead of your competitors by using social media's incredible power to capture the publics attention at scale. Now, the rest is up to you. Good Luck!

References

1. 10 Reasons to Use Instagram for Your Business. (2019). Retrieved from https://www.business.com/articles/10-reasons-to-use-instagram-for-business/

2. 46 Fascinating and Incredible Youtube Statistics. (2019). Retrieved from https://www.brandwatch.com/blog/39-Youtube-stats/

3. 48 Eye-Opening LinkedIn Statistics for Marketers In 2019. (2019). Retrieved from https://foundationinc.co/lab/b2b-marketing-linkedin-stats/

4. 5 Reasons You Should Be Advertising on Facebook. (2019). Retrieved from https://www.wordstream.com/blog/ws/2015/10/14/advertising-on-facebook

5. 6 Essential Steps to Increase Facebook Organic Reach. (2019). Retrieved from https://sproutsocial.com/insights/facebook-organic-reach/

6. A Deep Dive into Facebook Advertising - Learn How to Make It Work for Your Business. (2019). Retrieved from https://neilpatel.com/blog/deep-dive-facebook-advertising/

7. Everything You Need to Know About Instagram Story Ads. (2019). Retrieved from https://www.wordstream.com/blog/ws/2018/08/07/instagram-story-ads

8. Global social media research summary 2019 | Smart Insights. (2019). Retrieved from https://www.smartinsights.com/social-media-marketing/social-media-strategy/new-global-social-media-research/

9. How to 24X Your LinkedIn Post Views in a Single Day. (2019). Retrieved from https://neilpatel.com/blog/boost-linkedin-post-views/

10. How to Build an E-commerce Brand Using Instagram When You Have No Followers. (2019). Retrieved from

https://neilpatel.com/blog/instagram-branding-without-followers/

11. The Complete Guide to LinkedIn Ads: How to Run a Successful Campaign. (2019). Retrieved from https://blog.hootsuite.com/linkedin-ads-guide/

12. What is a Pre-Roll Ad & Why Should Marketers Use Them in Campaigns? (2019). Retrieved from https://instapage.com/blog/pre-roll-ads

13. Why do we 'like' social media? | The Psychologist. (2019). Retrieved from https://thepsychologist.bps.org.uk/volume-28/september-2015/why-do-we-social-media

14. Youtube Marketing Guide (2018 Update). (2019). Retrieved from https://neilpatel.com/blog/Youtube-marketing-guide/